The

Secret

to

College Success

Bruce R. Gibbs

Published in the United States of America.

You Will Learn Publishing
ISBN: 978-0-6151-9256-7

Library of Congress Control Number: 2008924043

Volume discounts and special sales opportunities are available with this book. Special opportunities can include re-branding of the book with corporate information or personalizing the book with an in-bound printed letter from your company or organization. To place an order contact the address below:

bulksales@mycollegesuccess.com

This book is dedicated to my two wonderful girls, Janae and Jayla.
May you one day find your success in the world.

And to my wife Janet for being the greatest wife in the world.
I love you.

What is the Secret?

What is the secret to college success? What is the secret ingredient that can help you make it from college freshman to college graduate? Can you just do one thing to guarantee this success? In reality, there are many strategies to help you be successful in college. This book shares with you those strategies in the hopes that they will no longer be a secret to you. This book will reveal, from a professor's point of view, what you need to know to be the best college student you can be.

You will also find additional secrets to college success on this book's companion web site, MyCollegeSuccess.com. When you see the @ symbol you are being directed to a section of the site that gives more details about that particular topic.

Enjoy this book and enjoy your collegiate life! You are in for the ride of your life.

Table of Contents

Part 1:
Arriving On Campus

Know Your Professor

Never forget this: your college professors want you to succeed. They want you to pass their classes and move up to the next level. So get to know these people who are on your side. And this means more than just learning their names. If your professors have office hours, pay them a visit. If you are new to a class, drop by, introduce yourself, and let the professor know who you are. But don't overuse the office hour or try to suck up to them; they know if you're being sincere. Besides, they are generally busy and overworked. If office visits aren't available, try sending an email to introduce yourself.

Professors like students who are motivated and look for those who want to be in their classes and want to work on projects. You may not always agree with the assignment the professor gives, but you should give it your best shot and strive to impress upon the professor that you intend holding up your part of the deal by completing all assigned work.

Professors have radar that easily spots motivated students. You can spot them, too. They're the ones who show up for class on time, contribute to class discussions, and turn in on-time assignments that do more than just regurgitate what the professor said. Professors want you to think for yourself and apply what you learn.

When professors see you are really trying and want to succeed, most will gladly help you. The ones who may not help are those who are lecturing huge classes and, for lack of time, just can't provide individual attention.

If you're having problems in class, talk to your professor *before* it gets too late. What's *too late*? The last week of class is definitely too late. As soon as you realize that you're falling behind or not understanding the class material, immediately pay your professor a visit, explain the situation, and see what he or she recommends. Getting to know your professor can help you more than you might think.

———•———

Want to see how a particular professor is rated by other students? Visit MyCollegeSuccess.com to see our list of rating sites.

Know School Officials

When people are starting a business, what's one of the suggestions they are given? To raise capital, first start with family and friends. Why is this? Because these are people you know. These are people who know you. They trust you, and they believe in you. These people have spent time with you and have a vested interest in you. This type of thinking cuts across all walks of life, even college.

It always helps to know people. At school you are surrounded by people who yield power. From the financial aid advisor to the dorm monitor, these people hold power that you may one day need on your side.

Get to know people on campus. This includes administrators, as well as faculty members. And, get to know people before you need their help. People can tell when you want something from them. If you wait until you need them, they may be less likely to open themselves up to you. But, if you take the time to get to know them in advance, you will have made a friend. Today you may need the professor's help, but tomorrow you may need your department's administrative assistant help. The key is to be nice to everyone.

Am I suggesting that you get to know people just so you can get something from them? No. Getting to know these people is a fun process. These people may become life long friends. I am not advocating these people could or would do something illegal or unfair. I'm saying it's harder to say no to a friend than a stranger. That's just a fact. So, get to know people, and help them when you can. If you do, it's much more likely they'll go out of their way to do the same for you when you need help.

—•—

Class on Time

Let's say I'm supposed to meet you at an agreed upon time and place, and you have a lot of information I've asked you to share with me. You are on time, but I'm not. Maybe I don't even show up. Okay, how would that make you feel?

Now turn that around and you'll understand how professors react when you are late for or cut class. By signing up for a course, you agree to meet with that professor at a set time and place. He has gone to the trouble of collecting a lot of information you need. If you aren't in your seat on time, every time, you shouldn't be surprised if his nose becomes a bit out of joint. After all, professors are human, too. Even though we may not seem to show it at times, every professor worthy of the title wants you to succeed in your college studies. We want you to excel, and we want you to graduate. Helping to assure your future success is the reason we teach. Trust me, we surely don't do it for the money.

By being on time for class, you tell the professor that you want to succeed. Don't be fooled into thinking that a professor who doesn't take roll isn't aware of who is and who isn't present – even when there are hundreds of students enrolled in a class. Your attendance and promptness record form the yardstick professors use to measure your determination to succeed.

I remember a student who came to see me during office hours, asking for help with some material she didn't understand. Do you think the fact that she was frequently late for class, seldom took notes, and hadn't bothered to even attend class on the day I covered the material she considered a problem had any affect on my attitude concerning helping her? Of course. So I did what most professors in that situation do. I suggested she find someone who had taken good notes in class and ask to copy them. No professor should be expected to hold private classes for students who really aren't eager to learn. On the other hand, most professors are more than willing to spend extra time with students who are doing their best but still find the material difficult. I certainly am.

If someone surveyed professors, concerning their pet peeves, I'm convinced that late-for-class students and no-shows would top the list. The reason for this goes beyond disrespecting the professor. A sloppy attendance record also shows lack of consideration for your fellow students who are there to learn. Who knows? The person sitting next to you in class may turn out to be an important contact a few years from now.

Let's also put all of this on an even more personal level. Have you thought about how it affects *you*? One of the major lessons we all learn from the college experience is how to deal with others and building successful habits. I assure you that, in the business world, arriving late for a meeting loses you points. Why? It's obvious;

people aren't eager to do business with anyone who is too disorganized to be punctual, wastes their time, and is inconsiderate.

Being on time in the business world and in the academic world means you need to go to bed at a reasonable hour and set your alarm clock a few minutes earlier. You should also allow for things beyond your control, such as a late bus or heavy traffic. If you get to class five minutes early every day, that's not five minutes wasted. That's time you can use to relax and look over the class material again. (I say "again" because, as a good student, you have already read the material. Right?)

Just keep in mind that professors want you to take an interest in their class material. I realize there is an occasional required course that doesn't give you a thrill. Still, since you are paying the tuition, you should want to learn the information that's presented to you. More often than not, a required subject you don't want to take is the very one in which your skills are weakest.

So get in the habit of being on time. In the real world, it's a habit that can double – even triple – your income.

——•——

Keeping in Contact with Family

I know you're glad to be on your own and that you're finally getting out from under your family's roof. You're an adult now, and you're living life on your own terms. This may all be true but you never want to forget or lose touch with your family. Take some time out of your busy schedule to call or send your parents a note. They will love hearing from you. And if you have siblings at home, send them a note, also. Family is too important to forget when you are away at college. I'm not advocating calling home everyday, but stay in touch with family members so that they know you are alive, well, and thinking about them.

Some of you may ask, "Why should I call home? They know how I am doing. Do they? Do they really know what you are going through at school? Your family is proud of your accomplishment of getting into college. They want to hear from you; yes, they want to hear from you even if you didn't ace that chemistry exam. Besides, you're not calling just to tell them about you. Don't you want to know how your family is doing? How are they getting along now that you're not there everyday?

How can keeping in touch with family make you a better student? It can help ease your fears. Connecting back to your home life can give you a feeling of security. Connecting with family gives you something familiar to hold on to in the midst of all the change that's around you on campus. Family can also give you confidence. There will be many things at college that you will feel you can't accomplish. But your family can encourage you to keep trying and keep pushing forward. When this happens, you become confident about yourself and what you can accomplish.

Keep in touch with your family members' lives. It keeps you grounded; it keeps you mindful of your roots. Like the saying goes: if you don't know where you've been, you really don't know where you're headed.

———•———

@ Want to send your family a note? Visit MyCollegeSuccess.com to use our note feature.

Homesick

Most students who leave home to attend college, especially for a campus that's far away, tend to experience some homesickness. Don't feel bad if it happens to you. It's natural to miss your loved ones when you are in a strange new place, surrounded by people you don't know. And just think, a short time ago you couldn't wait to get away from family.

One way to help your transition from home to college is to call home and hear a familiar voice. Or, write the folks back home a letter. These communications can help you to still feel a part of their lives while beginning a new one for yourself. Another way to deal with homesickness is to get involved in your school. Meet people, hang out in the student commons area, or meet people in your dorm's lobby. You don't want to spend hours by yourself wishing you were home.

If not dealt with, homesickness can lead to falling grades and even severe depression. So, while being homesick is a natural process students go through, you don't want it to rule your life and rob you of a rich college experience. If you feel you need to talk to someone professional about it, please seek out help. Your school should have counselors on staff or be able to refer you to one in the area.

Sometimes homesick students decide to drop out of school because they can't stand to be alone in a new place. Don't leave school without giving it a meaningful chance. This means more than a few weeks. It may take an entire quarter or semester to begin to feel comfortable in your new home. When you first arrive on campus, it may feel as if you'll never fit in or as if you'll never get used to being away from home. Trust me, you will. And, once you get over the homesickness, you're in for the time of your life!

—•—

Cheerleaders

At sporting events, cheerleaders motivate the crowd and spur the team to victory. Just as in sports, you also need cheerleaders to help you be a winner.

It's important to have people in your life who motivate you to do well in school. Your cheerleaders may be miles away or on campus. Either way, it's important to let the people who are genuinely committed to your success know what you are doing and what they can do to motivate you to pass a test or turn in an assignment.

Being away from home can be a scary experience. On top of that, college work can be draining and exhausting. So don't be afraid to pick up the phone or send an email, letting your cheerleaders know what you are experiencing.

It's a good idea to pick a few people and tell them you're counting on their cheering you on. Or you can keep their role in your life to yourself and just let them know what you are doing in school, then listen to their words of encouragement.

Okay, so now the question is who can be your cheerleaders? An obvious choice would be family members, including grandparents, aunts, uncles, cousins, brothers, sisters, and of course parents. However some of you might not be comfortable with the idea of letting certain family members know you need their emotional support. If so, move onto the next logical choice: friends.

Friends can be an invaluable source of support during your college years. While I recommend telling your parents when you are having difficulties in school, I realize it may be hard to break the news to them that you're failing a class or having a hard time with an assignment. It may be easier to talk with a friend who understands and may be able to help.

Members from your church or religious group can also be a tremendous support while you are miles away from home. Let them know that you wouldn't mind a card or a "care package" from time to time to help you remember them and to help keep you encouraged. These are people you may have spent a lot of time with. While they may hate to see you go, they really want the best for you and want to help you succeed.

In picking a cheerleader it makes sense not to pick someone who might bring you down or not support you. Sometimes people want you to fail. You want to be wary of and stay away from people like that. You want cheerleaders who are positive and have a good outlook on life. It's also possible to have a relationship with a good cheerleader change for the worse. If that happens, move on and pick a new one who will support you.

Having cheerleaders is important throughout your adult life. They help you keep going when things get tough. But it's also nice having someone in your corner when things are going great, someone to celebrate victories with, someone to motivate you to accomplish even bigger things. When people don't get support, they feel alone and tend to give up.

Can a person succeed in college without cheerleaders? Sure, but cheerleaders can make the college experience a lot easier. Throughout college and especially when you graduate, don't forget to thank yours for their support with a card, a lunch, or some other token of friendship. Remember: these people were there when you needed them. And you won't quit needing them, just because you have a diploma on your wall.

———•———

To Drive or Not to Drive

We all love to drive automobiles. In fact, some of us believe it's a constitutional right to drive (okay, that may be taking it a bit far but you get the idea). The point is we do love our automobiles and we love to drive. But for most people, cars are not free and this includes college students.

The first question you should ask yourself when thinking about an automobile is how are you going to pay for one? If you are like most Americans, you take out a loan for your car. This loan has to be paid back on a monthly basis. And unless the finance company has some college student special, this money will have to be paid back while you're in school. So if your car payment is, say, $300 a month, how are you going to come up with that much cash every 30 days?

The car note is only one item on the long list of expenses a car owner faces. Gas. Oil. Tires. Repairs. Insurance. Parking. Few college campuses allow you to park on their property for free. You'll have to obtain a parking sticker. Depending on the school, these are not cheap. Also, if you live in a metropolitan area, you will probably have to pay to park when you head for the downtown area or entertainment district.

Now let's talk about insurance. You've probably heard your parents mention this one. Insurance – especially if you are between the ages of 18 and 25 – can be expensive. Of course, you will want to check several companies to compare rates. You may also be able to become a rider on your parents insurance, if you meet the company's requirements. Insurance may be something that you do not want to pay for, but by law you have to do it. Besides, it will come in handy if you become involved in an accident.

Speaking of laws, many county or state governments require that you pay taxes on your property. And guess what? Your car is your property; so, that means you will have to pay annual property taxes on it to obtain a tag.

I have seen so many students get side tracked from their studies because they had to work or work extra hours to make a car payment or get a car repaired. (As sure as they have four wheels, they will break down.) You have to factor in maintenance and upkeep before you decide to own a car. How much you should factor in depends on the automobile you own, but it will probably be several hundred dollars a year. A grand is more likely, if your car has lost the bloom of youth.

If you have to get a job to pay for these expenses, then I suggest you think twice before bringing an automobile to school. You will have to decide if the job will take away from your studies or not. I personally don't recommend freshmen bring cars to school; all freshmen have enough to be concerned about. You don't want to add to the pressure by bringing a car onto campus and having to worry about how to cover its costs and the hassles of ownership. Some universities are now banning freshmen from bringing vehicles to school. They cite parking and space problems. So, if you plan to take a vehicle to school, check with the school to see what its policy is.

And yes, there can be hassles with car ownership. There will be someone who designates you as his or her personal chauffeur. And there will be someone who isn't covered under your insurance who will give you a hard time because you don't lend him or her your car. There's the day you can't find a parking space when you're due for a final. And on and on. Enough said.

While we are talking about transportation, let's not forget about mass transit. Large cities either have trains, buses, or a combination of them to move people throughout the city. Many also offer discount rates to students who take advantage of mass transit.

Depending on your needs, owning an automobile may be mandatory. But if you feel that you can get along without one, then I would strongly recommend postponing car ownership. At least, use the alternatives your freshman and sophomore years.

——•——

@ Visit MyCollegeSuccess.com for details
on student-friendly car insurance.

Computers

Computers are a lifesaver for many college students. However, you may not need to shell out the money for one. First, check with the college that you are planning to attend and make sure you understand what computer facilities your new school offers. No matter how much you may tell your parents you absolutely have to have your own computer, it may not be essential for you to purchase one. Most schools offer computer labs to students, and these labs are open late – many are even open 'round the clock. Some schools are now issuing laptops to students, which the students pay for through their tuition. But I will say that having your own computer can be of great help when you want to stay in your dorm room and work or go to some place where there are not a lot of people.

The main problem with having your own computer is also having the software that you'll need. The school probably has it for sale, since it's used on the school's lab computers. And depending on your field of study, software can be expensive. Many schools and software vendors, however, have student discounts for software; so, make sure you take advantage of any discounts.

If you plan to take a computer to school, I recommend a laptop versus a desktop. The laptop is portable; so, you can take it to class for note taking (no game playing). Also you can leave your dorm room with it, if your roommate is snoring and you can't concentrate while writing that 50-page paper.

You may or may not need your own Internet service provider. At many colleges, you can use the school's network as your provider. Check with the school's computer support department for details.

Regardless of whether you are taking your own computer or using the school's lab, always remember this. Back up your work constantly. That merits repeating. *Back up your work constantly.* You would not believe the number of times students have told me that they lost all of their work because their computer crashed. My first question is where is the back up? You always want to back up your work and save it in different locations. For example you may want to have a copy on your hard drive and another on removable media such as a flash drive. You can also use online services that will allow you to backup your work on their servers. Just make sure the backup is current. The backup file will do you little good if it's not. To make doubly sure you can recover your file if something goes wrong, keep two backup files. There is software available that can assist you with backing up items on your hard drive if you do not want to do it manually.

Another piece of valuable software to have, if you are bringing your own computer, is virus protection software. You could connect to the school's network using your computer, you may let a friend use your computer or you may download a file from the Internet. In any of these situations, you could contract a virus. Virus protection software can save you a lot of headaches and is well worth the price. Most fall in the $50-$70 range.

I advocate taking a computer to school, if you can afford it. My advice is to check out the school first before trying to convince your parents that you have to purchase one to graduate summa cum laude.

—•—

Visit MyCollegeSuccess.com for great deals on computers for students.

Living On or Off Campus

Whether to live on or off campus is a big dilemma for many college students because both options have their pluses and minuses. There are times, though, when you may not have a choice. If student housing is full, you may have to find an apartment or boarding house nearby. On the other hand, a few schools require all freshmen to live on campus, and I'm all for that.

Campus housing is usually not luxurious, but it does have its amenities. Some dorm rooms have computer network connections that allow you to gain Internet access from your room and to connect with the school's computer network. The cafeteria is right on campus; so, you may not have far to go to grab a bite to eat. And, getting to class may be a shorter walk from your dorm than from the nearest available parking place.

There's also the matter of cost. Staying on campus is usually cheaper than off, if you tally all your expenses. You save on gas and transportation. You don't have to pay for furniture, as opposed to an unfurnished apartment. Your food costs may be less because, once off campus, you have to buy your own food, as well as take time to shop for it and prepare it.

I recommend that students stay on campus at least up to their junior or senior year. As freshmen, students gain a lot by staying on campus. They become better acclimated to college life, meet other students outside of class, find it easier to become part of a study group, and are less likely to miss out on some campus activities. As a sophomore, you continue this experience and add to it.

Staying off campus may require you to have several roommates because rent isn't cheap. Monthly apartment rent can be over a $1,000 a month, depending on where you are attending college. Moreover, virtually all require a substantial deposit to cover potential damage. (Usually, a deposit is the equivalent of one month's rent.) You will probably not be able to pay all of this by yourself; so, you may ask a couple of friends to be your roommates and help offset expenses. This can open another can of worms because now you have to deal with more people than you would in a dorm room. Another huge problem is the fact that somebody's name has to go on the lease, and that "somebody" becomes liable for *all* the rent, if a roommate fails to pay, moves, or drops out.

If you plan to stay on campus, get your application in as soon as possible for student housing. Housing on college campuses fills up quickly. The same is true for overflow housing. Have your housing situation taken care of before you start your classes. You don't want to have to rush from class each day, for the first couple of weeks, trying to find a place to stay, while running up a huge bill at a hotel. I've heard stories of people who procrastinated and then had to wait in long lines, just to be told no rooms were available for them.

If you have to get a job to stay off campus, I recommend that you seriously consider your options. Getting a job can take away from your classes and assignments. It can also determine how many classes you can take because now you have to consider your working schedule. Is staying off campus that important to you?

Is it wrong to stay off campus? No, it's not. But, there may be a more opportune time to do it, say, your senior year.

—•—

Choosing A Major

Some of you will go to college, knowing exactly what you want to do. That's fine. Others of you will go not having a clue as to what you want to do. For now, that's fine, too. College is a time of discovery and learning. During college you'll be exposed to things that are totally new to you. You'll participate in discussions that you may not have normally been involved in and take part in experiments that open your mind to new realities. During this time, you just might reformulate your plans for your future. This is why, during your first two years in college, you are required to take introductory courses in a variety of fields. They expose you to a wide range of options and give you the opportunity to compare your chosen field with other career options. (You also need these courses in order to achieve a well-rounded education.)

The only problem with not having a declared major when you pick a college is you could pick the wrong college for you. For example, let's say that after taking a computer programming course at college you decide you now want to major in computer science. The problem may be that your college may not have a computer science department or it may have one that's limited, or worse yet it may not be accredited. In a case like this you would really need to transfer to another college.

Please don't feel locked into a major. Of course, you will research any field that captures your interest in order to make sure its opportunities are right for you. Also, don't feel you have to please your family or someone else by staying in a major you don't love. Even though your family members may have dreams and preferences about your career path, their overriding dream for you is happiness and fulfillment. Many people have led unfulfilled lives because they were afraid to change their minds, and major, in college.

Choosing a major involves a combination of factors. One is thinking about what you like. What are some of your hobbies? What do you tinker with at home? What do you dream about? If things that are electric fascinate you, maybe you should look at a career in electronics. Do you like writing computer code? If so, maybe you should look at a career in programming. Do you like spending time with elderly people or helping people with their needs? If so, you may wish to consider a career in social work. The key is to first think about what you *like* to do in your everyday life. Then, see if you could apply it to a career.

Another factor in deciding on a major is being exposed to it. In order to truly find out if you like chemistry or the law or journalism or whatever, you have to take a class or two in it. Being exposed to your chosen field will either solidify your decision or prompt you to change your direction towards something more personally satisfying.

The third factor in choosing a major is determining the economic outlook of the career. It's probably safe to assume your choice of career will be around when you graduate; if not your school would not have spent hundreds of thousands of dollars, even millions, to sustain a program for it. But, you do want to know roughly what type of dollars are possible for you to make in your career. To get this information, you need to conduct some research. Visit the library and look for reports that list data on salaries in the field you are considering. These reports should also be able to project future salaries for the next five-to-ten years. You may also want to visit www.salary.com to see what salaries they are reporting for fields you have under consideration. Remember: economics is not everything, but the rent (and your college loan) must be paid.

—•—

Having difficulty choosing a major? Visit MyCollegeSuccess.com to take a career assessment test. The test can help you determine your strengths and weaknesses.

Class Registration

One of the most hectic times you will have in college will probably be registering for classes. Sorry, but you'll go through it every semester or quarter. Each school has its own system of class registration, and some schools do it better than others. Many allow students to register for classes over the phone, using an automated system. Some allow you to register online for classes. Other schools require students to meet with officials involved with the registration process before signing up for a class. Regardless of the method, registration can still be a trying time, especially for a new student.

Some schools provide advisors, especially to freshmen, to help select classes. Their suggestions can save you a lot of time and help you to pick introductory classes that pertain to your major. Keep in mind when you are signing up for classes to not sign up for the hardest classes in your major all at the same time. You want to spread these classes out if possible. Some classes have prerequisites so make sure you know which classes you can sign up for.

To make registration less hectic, the key is getting started early so that you can register for your first choice of classes before they are filled. Once a class is filled, you will have to wait until someone drops the class before you can get in – and then that depends on how many people ahead of you are waiting, too. If a class is full, you may want to talk to the professor. She or he may be willing to sign a consent form that allows you to be added to the class, assuming your school has such a policy. Or, you may want to visit your academic department and explain your problem. If the class is required for your major, the department chair may be able to get you in. Still, nothing betters your chances more than getting an early start.

——•——

Roommates

Roommates can be a joy; roommates can be a pain. Having the right one can result in having a friend for life. After all, you've struggled through school together and, consequently, share a common bond. You also share your thoughts and dreams; so, you want your roommate to be someone who's likable; someone you can trust, someone who could develop into a true friend.

If you live in a dorm, usually the school selects at least your first roommate. Sometimes students are paired according to questionnaires they complete, matching their likes and dislikes. Usually, however, it's just first come, first served. It's also possible that you may not have the same roommate for each quarter or semester. People leave school, they may decide to move off campus, or they may wish to room with someone else.

Roommate problems that get out of hand can ruin a semester – even affect your school performance. That means these are problems that have to be dealt with early before they fester and become even bigger.

One of the major roommate issues is privacy (or the lack of it). When you room with someone in a space as small as a college dorm room, it can be hard to get much privacy. Privacy doesn't just include space; it also includes personal items, such as your food, clothes, toiletries, or your computer. You may see these items as yours, but your roommate may see these as communal property.

Another roommate issue that you may have to deal with is paying bills that are shared, for example a phone or cable bill. You may be responsible with your money but your roommate may not. Personally I don't recommend roommates sharing bills, but if you must you need to make sure both of you will be responsible enough to pay the bill. If not, the first month one of you doesn't pay his or her share, the service should be disconnected. You don't want to go on for months and months with unpaid bills hanging over your head. This will also affect your credit.

Another big roommate issue is cleaning. I've seen countless arguments between roommates when one was the neat and the other was not. One roommate may have his side of the room spotless while the other roommate lives like a slob. These issues have to be dealt with before they fester and become tough problems to solve.

There are several ways to minimize roommate problems. One is to talk to your roommate. Tell her about yourself. Explain how you plan to act as a roommate. Then get your roommate's point of view. It's a good idea to have a written agreement that states mutually agreed upon rules so that everything is clear and each of you knows what's acceptable and what's not.

Another way to minimize roommate problems is to contact your assigned roommate before the two of you meet. Before school starts, if you know who your roommate is going to be, write him/her a note introducing yourself and say that you are looking forward to the two of you rooming together. And, in your letter, include your address, phone number and/or email address.

If you simply cannot solve your roommate problems alone, then get someone else involved. This should be an impartial person, and many schools have someone on staff who can serve in that capacity. It may be the school's counselor, or it may be the dorm counselor. Some schools have forums for roommates to discuss and air grievances.

If you feel that you have exhausted all options and that you and your roommate just can't get along, then it may be time for you to find another. If this is your option, then follow the school's guidelines. Talk to the dorm counselor or the school's housing department about moving to another room. To prevent bad feelings – or at least minimize them – explain to your roommate why you think a move will be good for both of you and try to leave on the best possible terms.

By the way, it's possible that you may have more than one roommate. Many schools are experiencing a housing crunch and have to place three – even four – students in a dorm room or apartment. You should verify with your school how many roommates you will have before you arrive on campus.

I hope your roommate turns out to be a great friend, instead of a great pain in the neck. Your initial efforts at getting off on the right foot can make a huge difference in the outcome of your roommate relationship.

———•———

Find the perfect roommate. Visit MyCollegeSuccess.com to use a roommate service.

Gifts To Ask For

People will ask you, "What should I get you for going off to college?" Many times students say, "Oh, whatever you want to give me will be fine." While that can be a good answer, there are some things you will need more than others. The problem with my offering a suggested list is that every student will want something different. So, keep in mind this is a generic list that can be changed at will.

Gift Cards – Gift cards are like money, and money is always good to have. Many stores, such as Wal-Mart and Target, offer gift cards that shoppers can purchase as gifts. There are two types of gift cards. Store gift cards can only be used in the stores that offer them; for example, a Wal-Mart card could not be used at a Target store or vice versa; however, a card bought at one store within a chain can be used anywhere else in the U.S. The "use anywhere" types of gift cards are issued by credit card companies and can be used typically at any merchant that accepts credit cards. Just make sure you read the fine print on gift cards as some of them may carry fees. The good thing about gift cards is that they allow you to wait to get to school and then do your shopping, instead of having to pack the items for the trip. Make this gift really count. Buy something that will be useful throughout your college days, not a bunch of CD's or junk food.

Prepaid cell phone/phone cards – Prepaid phone service can be a life safer for many college students. Not having to worry about paying for phone calls is one less bill you have to be concerned about. This type of service can also help you monitor your call time because prepaid service can give you a set number of minutes to use. Phone cards are sold in monetary increments and are available in outlets, ranging from malls to convenience stores.

Refrigerator – No, not the large kind you have at home but one of the small ones that will fit comfortably in a dorm room. Your school may have these available for rent, but in the long run it's cheaper to buy one. The refrigerator comes in handy especially late at night when you are craving something to eat. If you won't need your refrigerator after graduation, you shouldn't have any problem finding someone who will be glad to purchase yours.

This book – No, I'm not ashamed to hock my own book. If you are reading a friend's copy, ask someone to buy one for you. Or, if you think a friend could benefit from this book, buy him/her a copy. I believe that the tips in this book can help you to succeed in college and have a rewarding time while there.

—•—

Get a more detailed list of items to take to college at MyCollegeSuccess.com. You may even find some specials on items while you're there.

Want to tell someone about this book but you're too busy studying? Visit MyCollegeSuccess.com and use our Send-A-Note feature.

Check with the "Authorities"

When a friend of mine was helping his son check out colleges, they did something I highly recommend. At each school they visited, they stopped a couple of students and invited them to have lunch or dinner with them. (They never had trouble finding takers.) Then, they spent their time with the students, asking questions. You can sometimes get a very different view of a school from students than the one you get from a brief and regimented orientation tour.

If you do this, ask your dinner guests about the school and college life. Will you need a computer? Will you need a car? How much money will you really need per semester? (Sometimes the estimates in college catalogs are overly optimistic and fail to include special lab fees, other unavoidable expenses, and having a little spending money.) What are the toughest subjects? (You don't want to cram three of them in one semester.) Ask about safety, bargain places to eat off campus, neighborhoods to avoid, and anything else that pops into your mind. Also, do ask my favorite question: "What should I have asked, that I didn't know to ask?" You may be surprised at how much useful information that one can turn up. Of course, two randomly selected students may not be the final word or they may have axes to grind; so, if you're unsure about your selection of advisors, talk with a few more students and see if you get similar responses.

Another bonus from the talk-to-the-students approach is, when you arrive at school, you will already know a couple of students, assuming that your dinner guests weren't graduating seniors. When you get on campus look these contacts up because they may continue being a good source of information and may turn into good friends.

—•—

Part 2:
Surviving On Campus

To Work or not to Work

One thing most college students have in common is a lack of cash. This is a real issue, and it definitely affects the college experience. Having no money can mean the difference between washing clothes or eating a meal. I remember many times during my college experience when I was flat broke and had no idea where my next dollar would come from. Because of this, many students look for a job. Sounds like the smart thing to do? Maybe. There are two sides to the job decision. Let's start with the positive side.

While working during college, you learn new skills, have new experiences, and meet new people who are often in your field. This can be advantageous to your career. Often employers are looking for college graduates who have work experience, as well as a diploma. They want to know you've at least had a taste of the real world. Fortunately, it's easy to get experience in your field because you have so many resources on campus, such as the career placement center and organizations in your field. Check them out.

The most popular way to work while in school is through work study programs, co-ops, and internships. Work-study offers great opportunities in that it lets you work (usually in a department on campus) to help offset the cost of your tuition. Also, it may provide you with some spending money. But all work-study programs won't be in your field. Many place you in school offices, residence halls, or cafeterias.

Co-ops and internships, on the other hand, usually relate to your field. They involve working for a company for a summer or for a semester or two. Co-ops put students into the environment where they will likely be working after graduation. This means you get real-world experience and become familiar with processes, work style, and company ethics. Also, co-ops and internships usually earn you credits toward graduation. Some pay cash to help cover your living expenses. Many companies have co-op or internship programs, and your school's career placement center can clue you in, concerning which ones you're eligible for and which ones you're not. For most, you have to have freshman and sophomore work behind you.

Working during college can also help you maintain a regimen and it can help keep you on schedule. Some students like the security of going to class and knowing that after class they have to show up for work. This helps them to schedule their day.

Here's the down side of working during college. It can take time away from your studies and the college experience. If you don't have to, don't work during your freshman year and possibly not during your sophomore year, either. My exception here would be if you were working part time in a job related to your field and you are actually gaining valuable experience or if you have to work to pay for your tuition. If working is absolutely necessary, don't take a full class load while holding down a full-time job. That's too much. It's better to take one or two classes a semester and really learn something than to fail a full load. That's a waste of the money you worked so hard to earn.

You want time to experience college life. You want and need time to soak it in. For most people, college is their first extended time away from home. If you just go to class and then head straight for work every day, you'll miss a lot the college experience has to offer.

Sometimes students have to work during college because they accumulate so many bills. I urge you to keep your bills to a minimum. Think twice before buying items on credit or buying items you really can't afford or truly don't need. There are some items you will need such as books. But you may not need that leather coat you've been eyeing or the latest computer on the market. If you keep your bills as low as possible you won't have to worry so much about finding a job just to pay bills.

Working during college can be rewarding and beneficial. It can also wreak havoc on your grades if you are not careful. Only you can decide what's best for you. But keep this in mind: You will have a lifetime of work ahead of you. Don't rush things.

—•—

Friends

Brian was a straight A student in college. He always went to class and paid attention to what the professor said. He participated in class discussions and met with the professor after some classes to discuss issues that intrigued him during the lecture. During his sophomore year, Brian became friends with an unruly crowd that neither attended class regularly nor turned in assignments. The group's behavior soon rubbed off on Brian, and going to class didn't seem as important to him anymore. As a result, his grades began to slide, and he was stunned to find himself suddenly on academic probation.

This scenario is played out hundreds of times on campuses, year after year. At college, you can choose the wrong friends. You know the type I mean: people who like to go to parties at all hours of the night, do not study, and do not attend class regularly. Students like these are destined to fail and are happy to bring you down with them.

I'm not advocating you becoming a loner. One of the best things about college is meeting people who may become life-long friends. College allows you to meet others with interests that are similar to yours and people who are totally different from you. You may have gone to a high school where you knew everyone's name. College isn't like that. You'll meet people from different countries, different regions of your country, people who speak different languages, people who may have different tastes in music, clothes, and food. From this myriad of people, you may find friends you can't yet imagine.

Be careful about whom you pick as a friend. A friend is someone who really has your best interest at heart and wants you to succeed. True friends will not hold you back or interfere in your striving to reach your goals. In fact, they will help you find ways to succeed. And always remember: your main goal in college is to finish successfully.

So, why are friends important to your success as a college student? They can help bring happiness. They can encourage. They can motivate. And they can be there for you when something goes wrong in class or on campus and you need someone to talk to about it. It's important to have friends. The support you get from friendship can really make a college experience special. And there will be the special ones who remain your friends for life.

—•—

Dating

The good thing about dating is that you spend time with someone you care about. The bad thing about dating is that you spend time with someone you care about. Yes, dating takes time. While there's nothing wrong with that, don't forget that you are in college to study and graduate, which also takes time. And just like your life before college, you have to learn how to juggle your class schedule and your social schedule.

Let's face it. When you were at home, you probably had some sort of parental control to keep you in check. You were to be home at a certain time, you had work to do around the house, and the person you were dating also had these restraints. Now, you are on your own and have to police yourself. While dating is certainly fun, it can also lead to disastrous results, if not kept in check.

Don't be afraid to let the person you are dating know when he/she is beginning to interfere with your studies. If the object of your affection truly cares for you, he/she will understand and allow you time to study. You can try to study together, but I recommend either studying separately or studying with a group. If just the two of you are studying together, it's far too easy for your focus to shift from your books to each other.

There can also be dangers while dating in college. For many

people, this is their first time being away from family and friends for an extended period of time. When people date, they usually get advice from their family and friends about the person with whom they are involved. It's good to get objective advice because others can often see things in a relationship that you may tend to overlook, both good and bad.

But when you are away from home, you may not have this protection. You may not have anyone to talk to about your relationship. You may not have someone to tell you when a relationship is dangerous or if the person you are dating is someone you really should leave alone. If you feel a person is dangerous, you need to end the relationship immediately and get the appropriate help to keep the person away, if necessary. Keep your family involved and let them know what you are going through. Also when you end a relationship, make sure you truly end it and don't send mixed signals that might invite that person back into your life.

Your college will most likely have professional counseling available, if you have issues about dating and need to talk to someone impartial. Ask for help, if you need it. Remember: the school wants you to succeed, and it has professionals on staff to help you meet your goals.

Dating during college can be fun. I met my wife during college. Maybe the same will happen for you.

—•—

Sex

Ah yes, sex. No book about college life would be complete without discussing sex. College is where a lot of students feel they can experiment with sex. There are no parents around, you feel you have your whole life ahead of you, and you are surrounded by people who seem to be thinking or talking about sex on a daily basis. So, what's a college student to do?

You will have many decisions to make as a college student. Having or not having sex is one of those decisions. And, it's a decision that can have life changing circumstances.

Let me explode the myth about safe sex. There is no such thing as safe sex. When you have sex you take chances. Period. A condom may increase the chances in your favor, but the bottom line is you are still taking chances. You are taking chances on pregnancy and the possibility of catching a sexually transmitted disease.

Often sex is mixed with alcohol. Students use alcohol as a way to help them overcome difficult situations or to ease into one. This is not a good reason to drink. If you need alcohol to be intimate with someone, then you're not ready to be intimate.

Professors care about your well being. They want you alert and attentive in their classes. They know life on campus can be tough.

They know it can be tough fitting into a new environment, with new pressures. They don't want you to deal with added pressures that could be avoided. Having sex brings with it added pressures, and you don't want these worries hanging over your head when you are trying to study for an exam or concentrate on a class.

If you need to talk to someone about the issue of sex, many schools have someone on staff to assist you. Or you may prefer to discuss the issue with someone at your place of worship. Many religious organizations also have people on staff who can counsel you in this area. And, let's not forget your parents. If you feel comfortable talking to them about sex, then please do. Trust me, they know a lot more than you think.

If you are thinking about becoming intimate with someone, remember that all it takes is one time. One time to get infected, one time to get pregnant. One time.

—•—

Drugs

For some reason, being away from home makes college students want to experiment with things. Drugs are one of those things. We all know that drugs can damage lives. We know that people can start with experimentation, get hooked and ruin their chances at a college degree.

More likely than not, you'll be approached by someone (maybe even a roommate) who asks you to try a particular drug. You will have to decide whether it's worth it to you or not to try it. My advice is don't. However, you are now an adult and will have to make your own decision. I can list all the evils that drugs bring, but my guess is you've already heard all that before; so, I won't rehash it. So, if someone does approach you, how will you handle it? That's worth thinking about *now*, rather than under the pressure of the moment.

Professors want students who are alert in class, not students who are strung out on drugs and can hardly commit to completing an assignment. You don't want anything to impair your ability to learn and grow. Neither do your professors.

A word of caution about going out. Be careful about leaving your drink unattended. When you go to the restroom or step away from your table, leaving your drink unattended can give some unscrupulous person time to place a drug in your drink, one that could render you powerless and unable to fight off an attack. This is a crime and should be reported if it happens to you. Be careful of the people you socialize with because on a college campus or in a college town, you will meet many people and some of them may not have good intentions. So, be on your guard.

The drug issue won't go away. You have to decide how you will handle yourself if you are in a situation where drugs are present. Keep in mind that illegal drugs are banned from college campuses. Many schools have strict policies if a student is caught with an illegal substance. These policies can include expulsion from the school. You tell me; is it worth it?

——•——

Alcohol

If you are just entering college, you are probably under the legal age to drink alcohol. Underage drinking brings havoc to college students and their families. Alcohol can impair your ability to think clearly, for example when you are on a date. (I don't think I need to draw a picture of what can happen when people aren't sober.) Some people make a point of showing you how much fun they're having while they are drinking, but they never show you the aftermath. The hangovers. The results of bad decisions. The embarrassment. The bad grades.

As a college student you are going to be bombarded by ads, students, and alcohol-sponsored events, all delivering the same message: *loosen up and have a drink.* When it happens, your parents won't be there to tell you to think twice. You'll have to make your own decision. And don't think that just because a drink didn't affect someone you're with, that it can't affect you, either. Different people react to alcohol in different ways. And by the way, there's this ridiculous idea being passed around that beer or wine isn't going to get you in the bad shape that the hard stuff will. Wrong. There's as much alcohol in a can of beer or glass of wine as in a mixed drink. Alcohol is alcohol, no matter how it's served.

Many schools have banned alcohol on campus and from

fraternities, sororities, and other school related organizations. This doesn't mean, of course, that these organizations never obtain alcohol and throw parties. Some do. Once again, use your judgment. Do you want to be around people who are drinking alcohol and getting drunk? It may seem fun at the moment, but wait until the morning.

If you ignore all the good advice you've ever received on this subject and decide to get wasted, at least don't drive. And never get into a car when someone who has been drinking is behind the wheel. Take their keys so they can't drive. Please, if you're smart enough to go to college, act like it and don't learn this lesson the hard way. Too many good people have lost their lives because someone drove drunk. I'm counting on you to do the right thing. So are your family and true friends.

—•—

Alcohol on campus is a serious subject. Visit MyCollegeSuccess.com for more information including links to additional resources.

Safety

One of the main reasons your family worries about you going off to college is your personal safety. They know all about the evils of the big, bad world and want you to be safe. A college campus is not an isolated island. It is not immune to crime. Instead, it is part of a city or town and is open to its inhabitants. If a city has a high crime rate, the college(s) in that area will probably also share that problem. Even when a crime happens off campus, it can invade the lives of a college student.

Many college campuses are proactive about campus safety issues and, among other things, have security teams or police. These teams are there to ensure your safety and the safety of everyone on campus by patrolling and providing assistance. Most schools also offer seminars or workshops on crime prevention and campus security issues. Attend these events to be informed about what's happening on campus and to see if there are ways in which you can help.

Before enrolling in a school do your research on how safe it is. Check the crime statistics of the school. Have there been any assaults on campus? What about robberies? Look at the city's crime statistics, too. Remember: you will be interacting with those who live in the city. While it's good to talk with someone about these statistics, you may also be able to get them from your school's web site. A good

place to check online for campus crime statistics is
www.campussafety.org. You also want to know about the security of
the college campus. Does the college have alarm/security posts
located throughout the campus? If so, you can use these to dial for
help in an emergency. It's also a good idea to know your local
emergency number. In some cases, it may be different from 911. Find
out how secure the dorms are. Check with the school to find out if
there is someone on duty in the dorm to patrol for safety or if there is
someone in the lobby or main area to greet and assist guests. If you
plan to live in an apartment, you want to ask about ground patrol.
How frequent are access cards for a gated community changed? Are
locks re-keyed when someone leaves the apartment community?
Wherever you stay, you want to ask how secure are the locks on the
doors and windows. When you go out, go out in a group. You are less
vulnerable in a group, and the group can also keep an eye out for
potential trouble to avoid.

Both college administrators and professors want students to feel
safe. If you don't feel safe, you can't concentrate fully on your studies
and enjoy college life. So, if you don't feel safe, let someone in
authority know about your concerns, make sure your concerns are
addressed, and if changes need to be made, follow up with the
authorities to see that they are.

—•—

Finances

Money. It's probably the toughest challenge to deal with when you are in college. It's not easy juggling bills and managing to have enough left over for some fun. I've been there.

No matter how little or how much cash you have, open a bank account. You need the experience of managing a bank account. Also, having one eliminates the possibility of losing a month's cash, if you lose your wallet or someone relieves you of it.

Most banks offer student accounts that don't hit you with big, monthly service charges. That's the good news. The bad news is, with student accounts, you usually have to take care of all your transactions at the ATM, and there's a downside to that. If you go inside the bank for a deposit or withdrawal, you may be hit with a small handling fee, a buck or so. And if you use another bank's ATM for a withdrawal you will definitely be hit with a service charge of one-to-two dollars each time you use it.

When opening a bank account, here are some questions you should ask. And don't think it'll make you look stupid to ask them because all banks don't operate with the same set of rules.

1. Does the account have a flat monthly fee? A fee for checks over a certain number written each month? Or a fee for every check you

write? If so, how much is the fee?

2. What's the penalty fee for being overdrawn (writing a check for more than is in your account)?

3. Is there a fee for using the ATM card at different banks? If so, how much?

4. Does the ATM card also function as a debit card?

5. Does a credit card automatically come with the account? You may not want this.

Let's stop the questions long enough to nail down a few definitions of terms.

The difference between a credit card and a debit card is a *debit card* deducts money straight from your bank account. This means you must write the amount of the purchase in your checkbook and subtract the amount from your balance (the amount of money you have left in the bank). Every purchase made with a *credit card* is the same as receiving a loan from the bank for the amount of the purchase. In the next chapter, we'll cover credit cards in greater depth.

The art of having money is being able to juggle it correctly. When you get your money you have to decide what you are going to do with it. Does most of it go into your bank account? Do you buy a book for class? Do you buy food? Do you go on a date? These can be hard choices when you have limited funds. When my wife (then my girlfriend) and I were in college, we used to have cheap dates at

Burger King. Sometimes we couldn't afford two orders of fries; so, we shared one. You'll have to decide which items on your list are the most important and do those first.

When you budget your money, no matter how little you may have, stash some away in the "rainy day" category. All of us have emergencies, times when we're faced with unexpected expenses. You won't be the exception to the rule. Doing this will also help you avoid the hassles of a math mistake that leaves you overdrawn.

You also have to watch your expenses. For example, if you have a phone and your bill is high every month, you may want to cut back on your calls. Yeah, I know, easier said than done. A great thing for college students is to use pre-paid calling cards or a prepaid cell phone. You pay up front; so, you don't have to wonder what your phone bill will be at the end of the month. Also, this gives you a set number of minutes to use, and you can budget your time according.

Handling money correctly is an art and if you learn it while in school you will be better prepared for the real world.

——•——

Some banks offer incentives for students. Visit MyCollegeSuccess.com for a list of student-friendly banks.

Credit Cards

Credit cards can get you into trouble. I know you didn't want to read that, but it's true. With credit cards, it's so easy to create a mountain of debt. On the plus side, however, a well-managed credit card is the beginning of a line of credit that you'll eventually need to purchase a house, buy a car, or obtain a loan for some other good reason. When your credit report is accessed – and know that it will be checked – you want it to show a good report; not one that's full of delinquent payments and high balances.

Having a credit card is new to most college students, and when something is new you tend to want to try it out. That's human nature. So when the new card arrives in the mail, the first place many students head for is the mall. It's like being in the desert and finally finding water. To a college student with no money, a credit card can seem like a lifesaver. But don't be fooled. When you are using a credit card, you are *borrowing* money from a financial institution. Read all the small print on the agreement you're given to sign *before* you write your name. Let me assure you it says you'll repay the money they loaned you *plus interest*. A lot of interest. And the amount of interest on credit cards is not the same; so, shop around.

Credit cards can become a deadly trap because, once you start charging, it can be hard to pay down the debt. This is not to say owning a credit card is bad. Credit cards can be used for good, and if you're the responsible type, a credit card can be useful. Responsible people with credit cards pay off their balances each month and do not charge items they cannot afford. Does that describe you? If you want to have a credit card or if a parent wants their child to have a credit card for emergency purposes, I suggest a card that has a low limit, such as $500. This way the student can not get into too much trouble if the card is misused. I also suggest parents talk to their children about what types of emergencies they can use the card for. A pizza run is not an emergency.

Do not, I repeat, do *not* place your credit card in someone else's hands to use. Learn from my experience. As a college student, I once loaned a credit card to someone I thought was a friend. When it came time to pay the bill, he was nowhere to be found. I was lucky he didn't stick me with a huge bill. When you lend your card, ultimately, it's *your* credit on the line – not the other guy's – because your name is the one on the card.

Beware of companies that come on campus, offering free gifts to anyone who signs up for their credit card. Their cards usually carry outrageously high interest rates; so, that gift is one you will likely pay for over and over again. I'm happy to say that more and more campuses are putting a stop to this type of solicitation from credit card companies.

You may have noticed that I keep using the word *card*, not *cards*. You don't need a pocket full of plastic. Most places of business will take the four major cards; so, one should suffice for you. Wait until you and the person funding your education are certain you're up to having more than one card before adding another card to your wallet.

The reason I'm so adamant about credit cards is I've seen what getting caught up in debt can do to a college student. It can rob you of a successful college experience. When you charge items you can't afford, you get caught in a vicious cycle. You have to either get a job to pay for the charges, or you have to work more hours to have enough to pay for a bill that could have been avoided. The extra work then cuts into your studying and preparation for class. In turn, your class work suffers, causing you to struggle to stay in school. Be smart and don't let this happen to you.

Remember: owning a credit card takes responsibility. If you feel you aren't up to the challenge, just wait till you've graduated and have a good job before dealing with the temptations that little piece of plastic creates. Trust me; it's the smart thing to do.

———•———

If you must have a credit card, get one with a low interest rate. Visit MyCollegeSuccess.com to get details on credit card rates.

College Loans

Most students pay for part – many all – of their college expenses. So, you may ask, where did they get all that money? More than likely, they got a college loan. And for many students, getting a loan can be easy. In fact, it can be too easy.

You can obtain college loans from banks and many other sources. There are even companies that deal mainly in loaning money to college students for educational purposes. The financial aid advisor at your high school or at the college you plan to attend can walk you through the steps.

The reason college loans are so attractive is because they usually have a good interest rate and, if you are a student, you can delay repaying the loan until you graduate. The keyword here is *delay*. If you borrow money, you are obligated to repay it.

Before you get a loan, read *all* the literature about it. Every word. And make sure you understand the repayment terms. Just because you've read all the fine print, concerning one loan agreement, doesn't mean the same terms apply to another. Each lender has a lot of latitude when setting terms. So, make sure you understand the repayment terms, and remember that it's a loan, not a grant or scholarship. The money you borrow will have to be paid back. Loan companies are increasingly cracking down on people who fail to live up to the terms of the agreements they sign.

Let's say you borrow $30,000. If so, you're expected to graduate, get a job in your chosen field, and pay back what you borrowed, plus interest. And that's a good plan. But, there can be problems with college loans. What happens if you graduate and can't find work in your field? What if you end up working as a sales associate at the local mall, while you are looking for a better-suited job that uses and pays for the pricey training you've received in college? Great job, so-so job or no job, shortly after graduation, your monthly loan statements will start arriving in the mail. How are you going to cover that first payment if you're just making enough to cover rent, utilities and food? Or what if, for some reason, you don't graduate? The money you borrowed will still have to be repaid. It's at this point people begin resenting the loan and the company that made it. If you wind up in this spot remember: *you* borrowed the money. The company just gave you what *you* asked.

Which brings me to my next point. If you borrow money for college, borrow as little as possible. Borrow only what you need for tuition and books. You don't want to start your life after college with a huge debt. Keep in mind that after college you may need to purchase an automobile, new furniture, a new wardrobe, and pay rent or purchase a home.

I recommend that loans be your last resort. First, exhaust all other avenues, such as grants and scholarships. Save your money and don't pay someone or a company to find scholarships for you. The Internet, the library, and your financial aid advisor are all you need working for you to make a thorough search. Also, don't forget about work-study programs. See what your school offers in this area and use caution. If you think working will be detrimental to your grades, then you may not want to use this option.

If you absolutely must obtain a loan, shop around. Make sure you get a good interest rate and that the company has a good reputation. Your school's financial aid advisor can check for you. And, if the advisor is allowed to, ask him/her to put you in touch with a graduate or two who have used the loan source you're considering.

Getting a college loan can be a lot of pressure for a person who may have never had the responsibility of handling a large amount of money. It can be nerve racking. So, before you sign for a loan, talk it over with your parents. Let them know what's happening and what you are thinking about doing. Who knows, maybe they have other options that you have not explored yet.

—•—

Need money for college (who doesn't)? Visit MyCollegeSuccess.com for a list of scholarships and financial resources.

Extra-curricular Activities

College life is packed with opportunities to do more than study. Sports, Greek organizations, clubs, volunteer opportunities, running for student offices: it's a long and appealing list. Just because these activities aren't factored into your grade average, doesn't mean they aren't great learning experiences and likely some of the best times you'll have at college.

Be forewarned though; extra-curricular activities require time, and 24-hours a day is all you'll have. So this is where your time management skills come in. If you are good at managing your life, you may not have trouble fitting a club or team into your schedule. If you are like most students though, you do have trouble juggling time commitments and need to level with yourself, concerning what you can and can't handle. Before joining a team, club or organization, get some answers. How much time will be required of you? How often are meetings held? Will you have to open your wallet to participate? What will be your duties? Having been president of a student organization, I remember all too well how much of my time went toward doing things in the name of the organization. And, yes, I totally enjoyed the experience and benefited from it. Just don't forget: the main reason you're in school is to get good grades and receive a degree.

You will surely have well-meaning friends who pressure you to participate in their favorite activities. Don't let anyone push you into joining or committing to anything. It's up to you to decide if you want to and if you'll have the time. Give yourself permission to say *no* to others and to yourself. It's okay to say no. It's also okay to say you may join later.

Consider if the club, team or organization you're drawn to connects with your career. Many fields of study have student chapters of professional organizations where you can participate, learn and meet new people. These experiences can help you in your classes and may even help you find a job after graduation.

Please understand that I am not saying don't participate in extra-curricular activities. They can be fun, and they can be important to you later in life. If you have time to work in one or more and want to, go for it. Some employers look highly upon students who have participated in teams and organizations while in school. But they check your grades first.

—•—

Assignments

At college, assignments seem to come in droves. Some involve a lot of reading, while others are projects or experiments. Whatever the type, make sure you understand what you are supposed to do; don't assume you understand. If you have questions about the assignment, ask the professor to repeat the requirements. If there's an assignment handout, make sure you get a copy. Also, ask other students to see if they have a clear understanding. You have to know what will be required of you in order to deliver and receive a passing grade. What you don't want to do is to turn in your assignment and find that it's not what the professor wanted. If you understand what the requirements are before hand, you are on your way to receiving a good grade.

If you are having problems with an assignment, talk to a student who has taken the class before. She or he may be able to offer advice and let you know the professor's grading style or what feedback he is expecting. Also, just talking to someone who has gone through the course can give you reason for hope.

Want to know a secret? Professors are not thrilled about grading. Grading can be a tedious process, and many professors grade 25 or more assignments per class. Think about the professor who is teaching 4 or 5 classes. This can add up to hundreds of projects and hours of grading, and not all professors have TA's (teaching assistants) to help them grade. Professors are human (really); so, they get tired of reading or seeing the same information from students hundreds of times. When you do your assignments, try to come at it from a different angle, while still staying within the assignment guidelines. Professors like to see students who "think outside of the box." Professors are in the classroom to challenge you to think. Show them you are challenged by turning in assignments that make them say, "This student really gets it" or "That's a perspective I've never thought of before." Don't just do enough to get by. Excel at your assignments. You will be rewarded for it by earning good grades and by gaining more knowledge about the subject. It's also a skill that can put you out in front of the pack when you enter the real worlds of business, research, art, etc.

———•———

Writing Papers

Throughout your college experience, professors will ask you to write papers. These papers will vary in length, topic, and content. Some will be fun to write, while others will test your limits as a student. Professors don't ask you to write these papers for their benefit or because they love to grade them. They give the assignments because they want to test your knowledge on a particular subject, to help you see a new slant on a topic, or to help you improve your writing and research skills.

When you write a paper, professors want to see *your* words and thoughts. They don't want you to regurgitate what's in the textbook. They already know what it says. Try to think about what the professor is looking for. If the subject has been rehashed often, try a fresh perspective and don't just give a surface level report. Really dig into your research and deliver an in-depth look into your topic.

If you are allowed to pick your own topic, check your choice with your professor before beginning to write. The professor may request you write a thesis statement or a short summary about the content of your paper. If this is not asked for, do it anyway and run it by the professor. You want to make sure you are on the right track before you sweat out a 20-page report.

Sometimes finding a topic for your paper can be difficult. You may wish that the professor had just assigned you a topic, but part of writing a paper is picking a topic and narrowing it down. To pick a topic, first think about what you want to research and learn. Or, think about a subject you'd like to voice your opinion on. Also, think if you will be able to find any information on your subject. Are there any quotable sources or references you can add to the paper? This is especially important if the professor requires references or a bibliography for your paper.

Thoroughly research your topic and take good notes. (Noting book title, author, and page numbers as you go can save you hours of work, once it's time to develop your bibliography.) Your notes become the basis of your outline. And yes, you do want to create an outline. An outline helps you plan your paper and organize your findings and thoughts. Word processing software, such as Microsoft Word, helps you use outline features in a document. If you have difficulty writing papers, you may want to pick up a book on writing papers for college. And, just a note of caution: please, please, please do not copy or buy a paper to turn in. This is plagiarism. Trust me; you will get caught. For more on this subject, see the section on cheating.

Some schools will issue students a writing guideline document that informs students how papers should be written for that particular institution. For example, it may state that all papers should be written in APA style, or that all captions should be centered beneath illustrations, etc. Make sure you read this document or if one is not issued that you ask your professor if she requires your paper to be written in a particular style. Trust me, you will hate to write a great paper only to have points taken away because you didn't follow the style guide.

Writing papers may or may not prove to be something you enjoy. In either case, it's an important learning process and comes with the territory. The harder you try to get something beneficial from it, the more likely you'll enjoy the experience.

———•———

Need help writing a paper? Visit MyCollegeSuccess.com for a list of college paper writing tips.

If you need access to cheap or free software to write a paper, visit MyCollegeSuccess.com for our resources.

Group Projects

Frowns and groans. That's what I usually see and hear, when I assign group projects. Students hate group projects. Some students just muddle through them; others absolutely beg to get out of being part of a group because they don't want to share a group's common grade. They think that they can more or less guess what grade they would make on their own but feel their grade average is at the mercy of the group, when the assignment is a group project.

There's some truth to that. So, why do we professors keep sticking students with something few like and many dread? Professors don't sit around thinking up group projects just to make your life miserable and jeopardize your grade point average. We do it because we know that group projects are an important part of your education and training. In short, they prepare you for the real world.

Problems that usually arise from group projects (during and after college) tend to deal with group dynamics. It's our job to help you develop group dynamics skills. After graduation, you'll probably be working in a group setting or will be involved in group projects in the workplace. Working with others should not be left to on-the-job training; you need the experience during college. Of course, everywhere you go groups will be different because they are made up of individuals. However, the skills you learn now can pay off for you throughout life.

When you are in a group, do your best. That means show up at all meetings, get involved in the discussions, ask questions, and do your best on the portion of the project that's assigned to you. If you can't make a meeting, let your group members know. Then, as soon as possible, find out what you missed. One of the major downfalls of groups is a slacker who doesn't show for meetings or doesn't carry his/her part of the load. And remember that there are no dumb questions. The one you're hesitant to ask is likely the same question that's on another group member's mind

As a group member, also try to help others who are not as outgoing as you are. This doesn't mean doing the work for them. That would only rob them of the opportunity to learn and develop their group skills. Instead, encourage them; boost their drive and spirit. When you do, you'll be honing your management skills, while giving others the opportunity of also shining. Professors look for this sort of interaction in the groups they assign … and reflect their approval in their grading.

If issues come up that the group cannot handle, let the professor know. Don't wait until it's time to turn in the project. When the professor knows there are problems early on, she or he can intervene – or at least can grade the project accordingly. This means the professor may grade each member separately or reduce the grade of the member not participating.

In short, group projects are a test of your ability to be a team player. No matter what your field of study, I assure you that the person who has the power to give you the job you want after college is looking for a team player.

—•—

Cheating

We all know cheating is wrong. We feel bad when we do it, but somehow we seem to justify it in our minds, saying things like, "I'll only do it just this one time," or "This subject is too hard," or the classic, "No one will ever know."

These are excuses your professor simply won't buy. To a professor, cheating means you don't take her class seriously. Once you get caught, that professor forms a negative opinion about you, a negative opinion that will be reflected in your grades or even in you being expelled.

If you find yourself cheating, you need to rethink why you are in the class. Think about why you are cheating. Is the reason a lack of study (which means you need to look at your management of time), or is it because of the subject material? Do you feel you aren't grasping the concepts? If this is the case, you may want to take an introductory class on the subject. For example, if Chemistry 101 is kicking your butt, you may want to take Chemistry 100 instead. Don't be ashamed if you have to drop a class because you believe it's over your head. It's better to have an understanding of the concepts than to risk cheating your way through a course.

You may also want to consider auditing a class, if you are having problems understanding the course's key concepts. When you audit a class, you don't receive credit for it, but you are allowed to sit through the class and participate. You will then be better prepared when you take the class for actual credit. Check your school's policy on auditing classes to see how auditing might help you.

If you cheat, you will eventually get caught. Students have come up with elaborate schemes to cheat, but most of those schemes eventually fail. Professors are not dumb. In most classes, professors can just scan the room during a test to see who is cheating. In larger classes, this may be impossible, but when professors see answers that are similar from paper to paper, it's a dead giveaway that someone isn't playing by the rules.

Some students have convinced themselves that copying the majority of a research paper isn't really cheating. Sorry, that's cheating. We call it plagiarism. And, plagiarism has become a plague on many college campuses. The Internet has made plagiarism easy and tempting. All students need to do now is copy and paste, and they think they automatically have a research paper. But trust me, professors can pick up on this, and will grade you accordingly. We know how to use the Internet, too.

Most schools have strict policies against cheating. Cheating can get you expelled. I urge you not to place your college career in jeopardy by giving in to the temptation to cheat. Trust me, it's not worth it. Besides, you're at college to learn, aren't you?

—•—

Exams

The dreaded exam. No one likes them. Yet, tests and exams are a mainstay of our educational system. An exam doesn't reveal whether or not you are qualified to pass a class. However, because they are often used for that purpose, you want to do well each time you take one.

Professors use exams to learn whether or not you comprehend the class material. This may not be a fair way to do it because not everyone tests well; however, since no one has come up with a better and more efficient system, you can count on being tested. If you are not good at taking tests, you may want to pick up a book that will give you tips on how to take tests effectively. I've seen these books help raise students' scores a full letter grade.

There are several types of exams that professors use, and one of the most common is the essay. Most students hate the essay exam. Their questions can call for short, though detailed answers or you could be asked to produce answers that each wind up being a page or more in length. With essay questions, professors want to see if you can formulate what was talked about in class in your own words. When facing essay questions, first relax and take a deep breath. Reread the question to make sure you understand it. Formulate your thoughts. Remember what was discussed in class and what you studied. If you don't know the answer, skip it and move to the next one. You can come back to the ones that give you trouble.

When it comes to multiple choice exams, it's true that some professors try to trick you. Among your answer choices may be one that closely resembles the correct answer, but is not one hundred percent correct. Or, you may be given a question with an answer that's so obvious, you choose the wrong one, thinking it can't be that simple. But mostly professors give straightforward tests. They just want you to answer the questions correctly and to the best of your ability.

If you have difficulty taking tests, talk to the school counselor. Some schools have programs that help students learn to take tests or they may refer you to an organization that works with students concerning test taking. Your school counselor may also recommend to the professor other ways to test you. Don't be afraid to discuss your learning problems. It's better to seek help early before your grade point falls.

——•——

Handling a Grade You Think is Unfair

What do you do when you have truly tried your best, but the professor gave you a grade that you don't think is fair? First understand that just because you tried your best and spent hours working on an assignment does not automatically constitute a good grade. Scores of students have come to me, saying they spent countless hours on a project and they feel that alone should give them a better grade. Sorry, it just doesn't work that way.

However, if you think that you have been graded unfairly, there are some things you can do to try to remedy the situation. The first involves talking with your professor about your concerns. Try setting an appointment with him, instead of just trying to catch him after class. He may have another appointment, or he may have another class to teach. You want his undivided attention. Also give him a heads up as to what you want to discuss with him so that he will be prepared.

When you talk to the professor don't be angry; don't start a fight. Also don't demand the professor change your grade. Ever hear the expression "you can catch more flies with honey than vinegar"? This certainly applies here. At the beginning of your discussion, find out what the professor was looking for from the assignment. If it's different from the assignment that he initially gave, then discuss this with him. If what you have turned in matches what he was looking for initially, explain that to him. Show him your assignment and point out where you addressed his issues. It is possible that he missed some of them.

Some professors do not believe in a perfect paper or project. They will always find something wrong or something that needs improvement. If this is his style of grading, you have to be prepared for it. When you turn in your assignment, make sure it covers all the assignment's parameters. If you complete your work early, re-check it for errors and fine tune it. Once you learn your professor's grading style, you will know what type of mistakes he will notice. For example, if you know your professor is a stickler for correct spelling and grammar, look carefully for those errors. Don't depend on your computer's grammar check. It's not as smart as it could be. If your professor wants you to explain your formulas in detail in order to show how you came to a conclusion, then you want to make sure to include that in your assignment.

If there was truly a misunderstanding of the assignment, ask if the professor will let you redo it. He may agree to this, but he may suggest that you will only get partial credit for the assignment. If he offers partial credit, take him up on his offer. Let him know that you are serious about your grades and that you are not afraid to work hard.

Remember to have a calm discussion. Professors are asked to change grades constantly by students; so, they have become, in this area, jaded. Understand that your grade may not change if you talk to your professor, but that talk may clue you in on how to ace his next assignment.

———•———

Distance Learning

One of the hottest trends in education is distance learning, which allows professors and students to be in different physical locations. It's not really all that new. It has been around for a long time, in the form of television and videotapes. Today, however, distance learning has moved to the Internet, which allows it to be interactive, an important change.

Distance learning can be a great resource for you and sometimes allows you to learn at your own pace, on your own timetable. For example, you can participate in a class at 2:00 a.m. by posting projects to the online class or respond to messages. Of course, there are some online classes that meet at set times, the same as traditional classes.

Some people see distance learning classes as boring or not intense. In some cases, this is true. But, distance learning has greatly improved and can be fun, interactive, and challenging. It all depends on how well the courses are designed. If you are thinking about taking an online class, talk to past participants to see how engaging it was for them. Did they learn what they needed to know? Ask questions to find out if you would benefit from this form of learning.

Nonetheless, schools, parents, and students need to realize that distance learning is not for everyone. Some people just learn better by being face to face with a professor and being able to see classmates. Distance learning classes take a great deal of self-motivation and, many times, require you to work on your own. They can also involve a lot more work than traditional classes. Professors may require you to examine other students' work and post feedback by given dates. This can be hectic, especially if there are 20 or more students in a class.

Distance learning can be used to supplement traditional classes. For example, instead of flying in field experts to lecture to a class in person, schools can offer a streaming video Web presentation of the expert, accompanied by an online chat room and additional online sources, such as articles on the subject being discussed. This enables schools to provide you exposure to specialized experts that would otherwise not be affordable to bring to campus for the benefit of just a few students.

You might enroll in a distance learning class if you want to take a course your school doesn't offer. If you do, before signing up for the course, check to make sure your class credits will transfer to your school.

As a past computer-based training designer, I truly believe that online learning has a great future in our education system, and I believe it can be a great tool to facilitate the learning process.

—•—

Getting Help/Tutor Assistance

There may be subjects in school that, at first, prove difficult for you to understand. That's okay because, if you already knew it all, you wouldn't need to be in college.

Understanding that college can be hard and challenging is half the battle. Getting help with your classes when you need it is the other half. Don't be ashamed to ask for help, if you are not grasping the fundamentals in the class. I cannot stress enough the importance of grasping fundamental concepts of a subject. Each new topic you encounter in the class will build on the subject's foundation and if its not understood, you will eventually be lost. Ask for help when you first realize you need it. Don't wait till near the end of the quarter or semester to ask. By then it could be too late. It is almost impossible to catch up a whole semester's worth of material in a couple of weeks. Also, you will not be getting the full benefit of learning and being in the class. You want to participate in the discussions, but you may feel inadequate, if you don't understand the foundations of the class.

Most schools have tutor programs to assist students. The professor may not always be available, and you may be able to grasp the concept even better from a fellow student or a student who has already gone through the class. Sometimes when students help other students, it can be a less threatening learning environment.

Again, the key to getting help is not waiting too late. And, guess what? Professors are impressed by students who are eager enough to learn and seek help when needed. I certainly am.

———•———

There are various online sites that can help you with if you have difficulty with a particular question. Visit MyCollegeSuccess.com for our list of tutoring or online help resources.

TV Time

The wonders of television! Who doesn't like spending time in front of the TV with a bowl of popcorn or some other snack? When I was in college, we spent a lot of time in the afternoon, watching cartoons, such as The Transformers and Thunder Cats. We loved it! It was also a bonding time between several of us guys, and it gave us something to talk about.

TV can be fun. It can also be dangerous, especially to a college student. With no mentoring or parental support nearby, TV watching can become a full time occupation, one that robs you of precious studying time or time you could spend on extracurricular activities.

I've heard stories of people missing classes to watch their favorite TV show. If this is your problem too, you may want to invest in a video recorder and record your show for viewing later. Set limits on the amount of time you watch TV and stick to them. Tell a friend what you are trying to do and ask him or her to hold you accountable. If necessary, ask your friend to come and get you out of your room to enjoy campus life. You don't want to look back on your college experience and say all I did was watch TV. They don't call it "the boob tube" for nothing.

If TV watching is a major problem for you, there's something you can do. Dare I say it? Don't have a TV at all. If you have to watch something important, you can go to the student lounge area, which probably has a TV, or you can visit a friend who has one. Even in these places though, set a limit on your TV time.

You also want to be careful of watching television into the late hours of the night. College students believe that they don't need sleep, but sleep is important. Your brain needs to rest, and so does your body. Professors want alert and responsive students in their classes, not groggy late show junkies. Trust me, you will sleep. Your body will demand it. The question is, will it be done in your room or during a class lecture. And, sleeping in class is not the type of message you want to send to your professor.

———•———

Student Discounts

Obtaining student discounts is one of the perks of being a college student. Using your student ID, you can get discounts at many places in the city where your college is located. Some businesses welcome college students by giving them a discount on goods and services, just because they are students. The merchants know that most college students don't have a lot of money and must spend the bulk of what they have on tuition, books, and supplies.

You can also get discounts from companies not located in your general area. Some web sites offer student discounts. National companies that want your business may also offer them. Some computer companies give educational discounts on software and hardware. The list goes on and on; so, whenever you purchase an item, ask if you're entitled to a student discount. The worst that can happen is hearing someone say "no."

The amount of a discount varies from business to business. At a restaurant it may be a free drink or side item. At a supply store it may be ten percent off. At a comedy club it may be half price admission. One of the best discounts is public transportation. Usually in major cities, students who take advantage of mass transportation are given discounts. So, as you can see, student discounts can come in handy.

How do student discounts help you to succeed in college? Any money that you can save is money you can reposition. For example, having extra money in your pocket can keep you from going hungry while studying late at night. Money can be hard to come by for many college students. So, money you keep by taking advantage of discounts can sometimes make it seem as if you won the lottery.

—•—

Advisors

According to the dictionary, an advisor is a person who gives advice. And, when you need advice, you don't want it to come from a novice. That's why most schools offer professional advisors to guide you throughout your collegiate career. I've said it before; I'll say it again: schools and professors want you to succeed. Anything that helps you succeed makes both the institution and the individual faculty members look good. So, advisors are motivated to steer you in the right direction. It's possible you may have different advisors throughout your collegiate experience. Where you are in your college career, changes in advisors' job descriptions, or a number of other factors can account for reassignment of advisors. Whatever the case, the advisors are there to help you choose the right classes, select a major or minor, assist with internships, or just hear you out when you need a sympathetic ear. As a college student, you'll have to make many decisions; so, it's good to have an informed and impartial source of information and advice.

While most schools assign you to particular advisors, you may be required to find your own. If so, ask other students whom they used as an advisor? Did they like that person? Did they receive helpful advice? Was the advisor available in a reasonable amount of time? Did the advisor initiate some of the meetings or discussions? (If so, that's a very good sign.)

If you feel you've chosen or were assigned an advisor who doesn't meet your needs, don't feel bad about asking for another one. This could result in replacing your advisor or having two advisors offering advice.

Many times advisor duties are part of an professor's contract requirements. Whether that's the case or not, professors like to advise students who are eager to work and learn. Many times I have deep, theoretical discussions with the students I advise. There have been times when a student was so eager, our conversations took place in a hallway or on campus, instead of waiting for a scheduled office time. Contact with your advisor should be by appointment; however, as an advisor, some of my best discussions with students have been the impromptu ones.

When you pick an advisor, pick one in your field of study. An expert in your field is usually a far better choice than someone from the outside. There may be times, though, when you want to broaden your horizons and choose an advisor who's an expert in a field you want to learn more about. However, do check with your department before choosing an advisor outside of your major to make sure this isn't against departmental policy.

—•—

Internet

As you already know, the Internet is a wonderful thing. You can conduct research over it, instantly communicate with people around the world, play games, and even take a lesson or two. The Web has changed our lives. The question becomes is it a change for the better or the worse? The answer to that question depends on how you use it.

As a college student, you are now on your own. There's no parental figure looking over your shoulder to see what you are doing on the Web. This is your independence, but it comes with responsibility. You now have to tell yourself that you won't do certain things – not because your parents are watching – but because of your own personal ethics. There are sites on the Web that include questionable or illegal content. As an adult you will now have to decide if you are going to be users of these sites. Pornography sites fall into this category. You know there are pornographic sites on the web that will beckon you to visit them. Some will entice you with promotions of free downloads and then ask you for a credit card. Also, fellow students may forward you links or encourage you to visit these sites.

Colleges hate these sites because they tie up computer usage and bandwidth. It's no surprise that many colleges have policies against using their computer networks for viewing pornographic material. My suggestion is to not visit these sites on your college's computers or yours. Porn surfing will only take valuable time away from your studies and from spending quality time with your friends.

You also want to be careful in chat rooms and using email. You've heard the dangers. Don't give out your personal information over the Web and definitely do not meet alone with someone you met on the Internet. Just as in the real world, everyone who hangs out on the Web is not nice; so, be cautious.

A word about email: please do not forward chain letters, no matter how well meaning. These letters take up storage and bandwidth space and are usually useless. Often they warn of a virus or a person who's in need of something or someone giving away "free" money. Before you hit that forward button check out snopes.com and urbanlegends.about.com. Both sites give helpful information about Web hoaxes and urban legends. It also gives related links for other sources that can help you separate fact from fiction.

Another danger of the Internet is time. Gaming sites, blogs, instant messaging, any one of them could keep you online for hours. Since you aren't going to school to become an Internet junkie, limit your computer time. Schedule the amount of time you plan to spend on the Internet and stick to it. Also try conducting research in the library. This gets you away from the computer. While I'm all for digital documents, sometimes, you just need to physically see the document in its original printing or package. Who knows, you may even make a new friend in the library.

The Internet is a wonderful thing. Just be careful how you use it and how much time you spend using it.

—•—

Studying

College is fun, but it's not meant to be a 24/7 party. There's a lot of hard, intense work, most of which involves studying. Studying is not an extra-curricular activity and may involve cracking the books throughout some weekends or pulling all-nighters. (Some would say, if you managed your time correctly, you wouldn't need to do this, but that's another topic.) You didn't get this far in life by not studying. That doesn't change at college. In fact, expect the work to be even harder because, at college, you cover more material faster. That math or language course you didn't take your senior year in high school now has to be covered in a semester. Also, in high school there was usually a family member who made it her or his business to know if your homework was done. But at college, you may be hundreds, even thousands of miles from home, with no authority figure urging you on. This can be a good thing. College teaches you to be self-sufficient. As an adult, you have to motivate yourself to accomplish things, and studying is one of them. The reality is that you will not have someone encouraging you to study. In fact, you may get just the opposite. You may have people knocking on your door, asking you to come to another party or to just hang out. You'll have many distractions, and your job will be to decide whether to study or to become involved in a different activity.

One thing that college is famous for is study groups. These groups can be as small as two people, or they can include an entire class. Sometimes study groups can be great. They are when the group's members benefit from each other, all learning more than if they had not had the advantage of the others' perspectives and knowledge. The flip side of that perfect picture is alleged study groups that are little more than social clubs, where people just talk and mingle. Pick your group carefully because you want to be in one that's going to help you succeed.

Studying also involves taking good notes in class. If your notes include what was discussed in class (instead of doodles), they help make study sessions more productive. While your textbook is of tremendous value, the professor may cover information that isn't in the text. Why? Because your textbook could have been published several years ago and not cover important current events, or the professor may want to bring in additional thoughts and discussion. A word to the wise: the bonus information the professor introduces is extremely likely to be on your exams.

You want to make your study time productive. This time is very important. You don't want to sabotage yourself by using this time to goof off or to just hang out with friends. Use this time wisely and learn something. And, be prepared if the professor calls on you during the lecture.

——•——

Study Areas

One of the keys to effective studying is finding a good location in which to do it. Don't overlook the importance of studying. We professors know when you are doing a good job of studying. And, we know studying is essential in getting good grades in college. As much as you may wish it, learning does not come about by osmosis. Let's start by listing places or situations that are not good choices.

Poor choices include:

- In front of your favorite television show

- In a loud dorm room or apartment

- Alone with your boy/girl friend (this is just asking for trouble)

- Jamming with loud music (hey, try soothing Mozart or Bach instead)

Now for some appropriate places for studying:

- Library

- Study areas designated by the school

- Quiet dorm room or apartment

- Dorm lobby (if quiet)

- Coffee house (if it's not too noisy and take it easy on the coffee)

- Serene setting, such as a park

- Empty classroom

Be careful about studying in a totally secluded area or where there is no security. While you want to study in a quiet place, you also want a safe one.

As a college student, sometimes my friends and I went to an empty classroom. There we had ample space to spread out our studying materials, and we kept each other company. Sometimes studying with a group can be good; at other times, it can be distracting. You have to decide what works to your benefit and what doesn't.

Effective studying boils down to knowing what is being discussed in class, absorbing what you read in your assignments, and taking good notes. Being in a good study area also helps.

—•—

Preparing for Lectures

Your classes in college will probably be bigger than the ones you had in high school. Be prepared for some classes, where the number of students can reach into the hundreds. While this may seem daunting, don't let it intimidate you. Just because you are in a large class doesn't mean you can't learn.

During lectures, professors like to see students become engaged in the topic being discussed. So, don't be passive. Participate in the discussion by giving relevant feedback or by asking questions. When you study, review your lecture notes so that you'll be prepared, if called upon in class, or so that you can add intelligent comments to the discussion.

Speaking of notes, make sure you take good notes in class. Some students feel they can rely on the textbook only and get all they need. Many professors interject their classes with additional information, which also needs to be in your notes for studying. The professor may quiz you on it. No rule says exams only cover what's in the text.

Some students record lectures on digital recorders for later playback. I'm not sure how good this technique works because I'm not sure how many students actually play back these lectures. But, if this does work for you, ask your professor for permission to record the lecture. You should also take notes along with the recorder to help you follow along when reviewing the lecture later … or in case something happens to the recorder.

One thing professors hate to see during lectures is someone sleeping in class. This is the ultimate disrespect. If you really want to turn off your professor, fall asleep during his class. While some could argue that it might be the professor's fault that students are sleeping in his class, this is not an excuse you can use. One way to fight sleeping in class is to get enough sleep the night before. Professors know that college life is hard but we expect you to stay awake in class to listen and participate. We don't prepare lectures for nothing.

Some professors handle sleeping in class in different ways. Some will ignore it figuring it's your loss for not paying attention, some will wake you up, while others may ask you to leave the class. Either way it's an embarrassment you'd be wise to avoid. If dozing off in class becomes a habit, it may be best to withdraw from that class.

Another tool in preparing for lectures is to read the syllabus and any other handout the professor gives. Most professors give students a syllabus at the beginning of the quarter or semester. And yes, they expect you to keep it until you get your final grade for the class. Many professors are now placing syllabi and handouts online so students will always have access to them. I always created a web site for my classes. On the web site were links to assignments, online discussion groups, syllabus, class schedule and other course-related material. I did this so students would be prepared and have access to this material 24/7. Also, as a professor, it was easier for me than carrying around stacks of paper. Read the items professors give you so you will know what's expected of you.

Since we are talking about lectures, let me say a word about cell phones. If you have a cell phone, turn it off during class. If it must be on, switch it to vibrate. And by no means, have a phone conversation during class. Remember, the key is to have a good relationship with your professor. Having a phone conversation during a professor's lecture is disrespectful and just plain rude.

Being prepared for lectures is a must for a successful college experience. Getting prepared for lectures takes some effort, but the preparation is well worth the time and energy spent.

—•—

Eating Well

When you were living at home, my guess is you ate fairly well. By "well" I mean you didn't go hungry. You probably had someone prepare your meals, or you had all the ingredients to prepare your own. Well, in college it's a little different. At some schools, three meals a day in the college cafeteria are covered by your tuition. At a few, even snacks are included in the total package. However, a cafeteria meal ticket is usually optional. Some schools have an on-campus cafe and/or fast food restaurant that offers additional options (usually on a pay-as-you-go basis). My point is, during your campus tour, ask about food sources on and off campus. No two schools offer you exactly the same options.

I know this may sound stupid but take the time to eat. College class schedules can be hectic, and it may sometimes be hard to squeeze in time for breakfast, lunch, and dinner. But, remember that you need your nutrition. Food helps you keep going throughout the day. If you are like most college students and are perpetually broke, then you definitely want to eat while the cafeteria is open. Missing meals can also be hazardous to your health. For example, according to health experts, missing meals can lead to being hypoglycemic.

By the way, try to eat nutritious meals. Soda, sweets, and pizza are not the three major food groups. Even your cast iron stomach needs fruits and vegetables. Just because you're not home doesn't mean you should eat junk food all day.

If you live in an apartment and plan to cook your own meals, here's a system that may work for you. Set aside half a day on the weekend and cook a number of different foods. Then freeze what you cook in single portions, which you can thaw, as needed. It can save money, save time, and be a fun thing to do with a roommate or friend.

How does eating well help you in school? It helps you concentrate. Professors don't want students in class whose minds are wandering or operating in low gear. Nutritious food also helps the brain to function when studying, taking exams, or just trying to make the right impression on someone. When people say, "You are what you eat," they aren't kidding.

—•—

Illness

Your family will worry about your safety and health while you are away from home. Try to take care of yourself because you are now on your own, without a parental figure to keep an eye on your health.

Many college campuses have student health centers. These centers are staffed with qualified medical personnel who should be able to help when you are sick. Check the school's web site to learn more about the facility and the staff.

If your illness is serious or if you are not getting better, inform your parents. Please don't keep them in the dark about a serious medical problem. They have the right to know what's going on with you. If you have a pre-existing illness that requires medical attention, make sure the school's health center is aware of your needs and that they have the necessary equipment or medication to serve you. You don't want to wait until an emergency for them to find the equipment or medication that could save your life.

If you are feeling sick, don't wait too long to see a health care professional. You may have caught a disease that you could possibly be spreading. The sooner you get help, the better you will feel, and you may stop or reduce the chance of spreading a nasty bug throughout campus.

Sickness can keep you out of a class. And in college courses, missing a couple of class sessions can be hard to make up because so much material gets covered while you are absent. If you have to miss class, make sure you have someone who can tell you what was covered and can share detailed notes with you. If your school tracks attendance, let your professor know why you were absent. If your illness will keep you out of class for several sessions touch base with the professor and let her know what's going on and to get upcoming assignments. And if you can work on assignments while you are recovering please do so and have your work turned in by a friend or classmate. This way the professor knows you are trying and that you want to succeed in the class. And by all means, get well soon.

—•—

What If You Get A Bad Professor?

What if you get a professor who you feel isn't teaching what you need to know? It would be wrong for me to tell you that every college professor believes that teaching is their life's work, and that they are totally committed to it. Some professors are burned out. Others may not be as knowledgeable in the subject matter as they should be. Whatever the reason, all professors are not the same. So, what do you do if you get one of these professors? Try to switch to another class taught by a different professor. Of course, you want to make sure there's room for you in the other class before you switch. Another possibility is to talk to your professor. Explain to him that you would like to get more out of the class than what he's teaching. He may refer you to additional sources such as faculty or a professional who can give you the help you are looking for. This still doesn't excuse the professor for not being prepared to fully teach a class, but at least you can make the best of a bad situation and still learn what you need, if you take the appropriate action.

It is not wrong to speak out. There have been many changes at colleges because students spoke up and if necessary, protested. As a student you are a powerful force for change. If you believe you are not getting what you want from a class you need to let someone know it. And, that someone should be a person in authority. If, after talking with your professor, you still don't feel you are being taught what was promised, request a meeting with the department chair. You may want to precede your meeting with a letter addressed to him/her that explains your issues to the chairperson. It is at this level that changes are usually made. The change may be a transfer to another class. Or, it may be having a special tutor. Whatever the change, make sure it meets with your needs for a successful college experience.

You are a customer and the school is a business. As a customer, you pay for services that should be rendered to you in a timely and professional manner. Your services at a college are your classes. You pay for these classes, and they should meet the requirements that are stated in the school's catalog. If a class description states you will learn the foundations of Java programming, that's what you should be taught.

Professors should be held to high standards. If they are teaching a subject, they should be knowledgeable in it. In fact, some schools require that professors continue to work in their field of expertise while teaching. This ensures that they are current in the field and in turn, can bring their experience into the classroom. Many schools go through a rigorous process of finding and preparing instructors, making sure they are qualified to teach in their area of expertise. I want to assure you that in most cases your professor will be capable to teach your class and will give you the materials you need to succeed in the class.

I hope you never get an unqualified professor. You may not agree with the professor, you may think he has an unorthodox teaching style, or you may not even like him. Nonetheless, ask yourself this question: *Are you being taught what was described in the class description?* If so, work hard in the class; if not, work hard to change to another class or change the class you are in.

——•——

What If College Is Not For You?

After being in college for a while, you may decide that college is not for you. However, this is a decision that you should not make lightly. College is hard work, and you should not leave it just because it's hard and challenging. If it were easy, you wouldn't need to take an entrance exam to get into college. So, if this is your struggle, work through it instead of giving up.

But let's face it; college is not for everyone. If your heart is not in it, if you are constantly getting failing grades, if your overall GPA consistently hovers in the 1-point-something range (or whatever your school considers failing), it may be time for a change.

There may be times when you will feel like dropping out of college. You may go through an entire semester feeling like you want to quit. This is not an adequate reason for giving into your impulses. All students have their bad days, weeks, and semesters. You may even have a semester where you are failing. Don't let this be the reason you leave school. Don't throw everything you worked so hard for away for one bad semester. Try to keep things in perspective.

Professors want students who are eager to learn, who want to be in school, whose hearts are really into learning. They want students who are really trying to succeed. Most will work with students who are struggling and having a difficult time grasping class concepts.

You know if you are trying at your schoolwork. (So does your professor.) If you are goofing off, never turning in assignments, and not going to class, you are wasting your (or your parents') money, your time, and the professor's time. A student with a profile like this needs to take a serious look at his future and decide where he wants to go and how he plans to get there. If college doesn't seem to be the answer, then a tough decision needs to be made.

If you are thinking about dropping out, first talk to several people. Talk with your parents, your school's counselor, and your college department's chairperson. Let these people know what's going through your head. While they may not agree with what you have in mind, they may be able to help you make a more informed decision.

I wrote this book to help students stay in college and succeed in their dream of achieving a college degree, and I urge you to stay in college and finish what you started. But, if your heart isn't in it, move on. Perhaps you'll be one of those people who returns to college several years later, with a determination to get that degree. College is important and can enrich your life in ways you cannot yet understand. I truly hope you stick with it, apply yourself, and succeed.

—•—

Part 3:
Succeeding On Campus

Don't be Afraid to Fail

Frequently, I see students who are afraid to try something new. They reason the project won't be a success or that they won't be able to complete it the way they would like. So instead of trying, they don't start the project or fail to put their all into it.

Here's what's wrong with that picture. If you refuse to try something, you'll never know if you have what it takes to succeed. It could have been something the professor loved. Also, look at it this way: by not trying, you guarantee yourself a failing grade. When you don't put your all into a project, you create a self-fulfilling prophecy (and you thought you weren't psychic). A halfhearted approach assures you a disappointing outcome. Also, the professor will be able to tell whether or not you really put the time and effort into the project. Even more important is how you feel about yourself and the amount of work you put into the project.

It's okay to be afraid. The people who ultimately succeed usually were afraid they might not. The difference is they tried. Fear didn't paralyze them, keeping them from doing what they wanted or needed to do. Professors will give you projects that will push your creative juices to the edge. That's what you want. You want to be challenged, not just spoon fed.

When something comes along that you are afraid of, decide

whether or not you really want to do it. If you do, don't let fear stop you. If you really have a problem with fear, consider picking up a book or two on the subject. You may not receive a high grade on every project or assignment you attempt. Just try and learn from your mistakes. That's how successful people succeed at life.

—•—

Procrastination

Have you ever waited until the last minute to write that paper or complete that project? Procrastination is the evil that every college student has to deal with. If you can kick this beast while in college, you'll be ahead of many people in your adult life. Many times I've seen students wait until the day a report was due to begin writing it. I've heard excuses like, "I do my best work at the last minute" or "The assignment is so easy I can wait until the night before it's due to do it." While you may finish an assignment ten minutes before class, trust me, if you get it done ahead of time you will feel better about the project and you will have more time to improve it. As a professor I have seen many projects that, if the student spent more time on them, they could have been so much better. Completing a project ahead of time could mean the difference between a "C" and an "A".

When I asked one student who was late starting a project to show me what progress he had made, he said he was still "thinking" about possible project topics. The next week, when I checked with him, he was just beginning to create an outline, which meant he was already behind schedule. I urged him to stop procrastinating and to make some head way on the project. He said he wasn't procrastinating and was busy working on the assignment. What he was doing was busywork, not productive work. He never turned in that project, and his grade suffered for it. It's easy to hide procrastination from yourself by doing busywork.

Many professors will not take a project after the due date. And they don't take "computer problems" as an excuse. (Alleged computer problems have become the college equivalent of "the dog ate my homework.") There are too many ways to avoid computer problems for them to be acknowledged as a valid reason for being late on an assignment. Properly backing up your work is part of your responsibility. If you start early on your assignment, you'll have time to properly back up your work (this also means in different physical locations), and if you really lose work due to computer problems, you'll have your back up file to continue your work.

Trust me, when I say that procrastination will keep you from doing your best work. Yes, you may get the work done just in time, but it won't be your very best. Start early, even if it's with only a few ideas. Jot down some thoughts just to get started. Once you begin the project or assignment, it will become easier to continue. You may hit a few bumps or have a mind block or two, but if these come after you get started, it won't be hard to get back to work on the project. Learn from the mistakes of many. Procrastination can keep you from doing your best work.

—•—

Public Speaking

Most likely, you will be asked to make a speech or give a presentation at some point during your college career. Don't run from this opportunity. Accept the challenge. Making speeches and presentations in college will help you in your professional career. You may be able to list these presentations on your resume (i.e. speaking at an organization meeting, etc.). Even better, you will have accomplished a goal many people only dream about: standing before people who recognize you as an informed source on a subject of importance.

Making a speech is high on many people's fear list. And that's okay. Notice that I did not say don't be afraid of making a presentation. I said do not *run* from it. Some believe fear can help you do an even better job. It's okay to be afraid of public speaking, but don't let that fear keep you from accomplishing your goal. If you get the chance to make a speech, do it.

Your public speaking may not just be in class. You may be campaigning for a student political office, or you may be asked to speak at a community event or organizational meeting in your field. Your school may also have open forums for students to voice their thoughts and opinions to the school's administration. Take these opportunities to say what's on your mind and use them to sharpen your public speaking skills.

There are things you can do to help you with your fear of public speaking. First, plan your speech. You may want to write it out entirely, or you may want to outline it. Do whatever works for you. Having something on paper sometimes helps to calm the fears of speakers.

Practice, practice, practice. This is especially true if you are making a formal presentation. You want to practice what you are going to say. You owe it to your audience to present yourself in the best possible way. Be energetic. Be powerful. Pick up a couple of books about public speaking for tips that can help you face your fears.

You may also want to take a class on public speaking. This will force you to speak and test your speaking skills in a non-threatening environment. If you feel that you did not do as well as you had hoped on your presentation, don't feel bad. Just try it again.

Another type of class you may wish to take is acting class or a drama class. For some people, this has helped them with their fear of speaking in public. While public speaking is not necessarily acting, acting does allow you to get comfortable with speaking in front of an audience. Who knows? You may end up in an entirely different career.

—•—

Time Management

The managing of your time will be one of the hardest things you will have to master at college. If you can conquer this task effectively, you will not only help your college career tremendously, you will also give a big boost to your future professional career.

As a college student, you'll be pulled in many directions. People will ask you to join their organization or club, fraternities or sororities may want you to join them, a group may want you to run for a school office, or you may be offered a part-time job. Oh yeah, let's not forget you have classes also.

A student of mine was doing well in class, doing good work, and earning good grades. Then she became involved in several student activities, such as student government and organizational clubs. On top of that she took a part time job. There's nothing wrong with any of those things, as long as they aren't made priority number one. Unfortunately, the activities and job began to dominate her life. As a result, her grades suffered. After making some tough decisions concerning the management of her time, she began to get her life back in order and her grades up again.

One way to help you maintain a schedule is to get yourself a scheduler or calendar. In it, record what you will do for the current and following weeks. After a while you can look back through it to see what you had accomplished … and where the snags are. Your main purpose in school is to take classes and pass them. That's what your time schedule should reflect. So, your schedule should have your class times marked, as well as the times you are to study for those classes.

The type of scheduler you use is up to you. Some people like the paper schedulers, others like PDA devices, while others may have a scheduler on their computer. Whatever works for you is the way to go.

—•—

Dream

How do car manufacturers sell their cars? Many show successful people doing what they really love, such as camping or skiing. They show people getting away from it all by driving on open roads that lead to excitement or mystery. What's happening here is the manufacturers are selling a dream. They want you to picture yourself in the situation, saying to yourself, "If I had that car, then I could live that kind of life." And the strategy works. Automakers sell millions of cars each year by enticing people to want the dream.

Dreaming is powerful. It can help you to see what you want. This is why I encourage daydreaming (though not during my classes). Dreaming can show you what's possible and what the outcome can be. Many people who are in show business dream of the day when they will win an Academy Award. This dream helps them to hone their craft, to better themselves. This same technique can work for you.

Four years can seem like a long time. And four years in college can definitely seem long and hard. To help you make it through those years, dream about life after graduation. What will you do, where will you go, who will you spend the majority of your time with, will you get married, etc.? If life after graduation seems too far off, then dream about your next year. What classes will you take, whom will you meet, will you run for student office?

Dreaming can get people through bad or tough situations. People in trying times have gotten through them by looking to tomorrow or a better day. It's that hope of a better time to come that keeps them going. You are on your road to a better day. While a college degree doesn't write your ticket to a happy life, it can give you better odds of achieving some of the goals you may have, such as getting a job or starting a business.

Dreaming, though, should not be used as a form of escapism. You will have problems and difficult times in college. You have to deal with these issues. You can't just dream them away. You also cannot – nor should you – run from your problems. Face them head on. By dealing with problems now, you will be better equipped to achieve your after-graduation dreams.

While it's okay to dream, dreaming without action is dangerous. Yes, you can dream about life after college, but you first have to finish college. Don't get so caught up in your dreaming that you forget about why you are in school. Dreaming without action can lead to misdirected, unfulfilled lives. Many people dream about a great life but fail to do the things necessary to turn their dream into reality. Stay away from that trap. Do dream, but work toward your dream to make it a reality.

—•—

Have Fun

You've heard the adage, "all work and no play makes Jack or Jane a dull person." Well, the same is true for college students. It's easy to forget to take time out to relax when you are scheduling projects and research papers. While you should spend ample time studying, taking a break and relaxing is important. If you don't have a little fun, you will eventually burn out. You may be surprised that an professor is saying this, but we believe students deserve time to "let their hair down."

When you do have fun, make sure it is the type that won't land you in jail or in the hospital. Take a break from your studies by spending time with your friends. See a movie, go on a short trip, or attend a school sporting event. Do something that will take your mind off your course work for a while. If you are on the computer or Internet 24/7, you should spend some relaxing time away from the computer. There is a world beyond the Internet; go out and enjoy it.

Remember that relaxation needs to be done in moderation. Too much can result in a lack of studying, and you don't want to reduce the amount of time you apply to your courses.

Part of attending college is what you experience outside of the classroom and away from your books. You don't want to miss college life by always being cooped up in your dorm room or a library. It is possible that what you experience outside of the classroom can be applied to what you are studying in a class. Have a social life and mingle with your fellow students. The occasional break will do you good.

———•———

Graduate

The reason you enter college is to leave it as a college graduate. All your education, from kindergarten up to now, apexes at this moment. From the day you were born, your parents probably dreamed about the day you would graduate from college. Many people invest much time and money into making that moment happen. So, it's not just your success. It's also shared by your family, your friends, your teachers, and people you've met along the way. College graduation is a crowning achievement. And it's not an achievement to be taken lightly.

You have to work to make college a success: it doesn't just happen. Believe me, it takes work. But, you can do it. With your drive, tenacity, and willingness to succeed, you can overcome the obstacles you'll face at school. Remember: millions have, and you can join their ranks.

If you get down or discouraged, pick up this book and flip through its pages to find the topic on which you need encouragement. When you get discouraged don't give up. Keep fighting, and you will see the mortarboard at the end of the tunnel.

Yes, you can finish college successfully. And when you finish, thank those who have helped you. Send a note to your elementary or high school teacher thanking them for getting you to this point.

Thanks friends who encouraged you. Thank college professors. And send a special thank you to your parents who may even be footing the bill for your college education. Show them you appreciate them and their belief in you. Hang in there and your dream of college success will come true. Reading this book gives you a head start. Always remember, you can do it!

—•—

About the Author

Bruce Gibbs has taught classes at the University of Washington, the Art Institute of Atlanta, Gwinnett Technical College, Georgia Perimeter College, and the University of Phoenix. He has worked as a consultant for a Big 5 consulting firm and has spoken at several national conferences. If you wish to contact Mr. Gibbs for a speaking event you can contact him at MyCollegeSuccess.com.

Share Your Story

If you would like to share with me your college experience or how this book has helped you, please contact me via our web site at MyCollegeSuccess.com.

www.ingramcontent.com/pod-product-compliance
Lightning Source LLC
Chambersburg PA
CBHW021011090426
42738CB00007B/749